Check out these other exciting
▼ STECK-VAUGHN Mysteries!

Who's at th
Get
MOD

A trip into the wil
See why in
TERROR TRAIL

Here's a job that will really haunt you.
Check out
GRAVE DISCOVERY

It's time to face the music! Take a look at
SEE NO EVIL

Who's *really* behind the wall?
See for yourself in
A BONE TO PICK

Who's calling? Get the answer, read
PLEASE CALL BACK!

Somebody's inside . . . but nobody should be.
See who in
ANYBODY HOME?

Someone's planning an *un*welcome.
Find out more in
HOME, CREEPY, HOME

Shop . . . until you drop!
Read all about it in
BUYING TROUBLE

ISBN 0-8114-9300-8

4 5 6 7 8 9 98

Produced by Mega-Books of New York, Inc.
Design and Art Direction by Michaelis/Carpelis Design Assoc.

Cover illustration: Don Morrison

STOLEN BASES

by Alex Simmons

interior illustrations by
Frank Mayo

STECK-VAUGHN
COMPANY

CHAPTER 1

"Mike, look out!" Laurie Chen shouted. Her warning came too late. She heard Mike Stevens grunt. Then he hit the ground hard.

For a moment everything was silent. Then Mike stood up and rubbed his leg. Sweat poured down his face. The umpire shouted, "Ball four! Take your base!"

Half the crowd in Carver High's baseball stadium began booing at the pitcher.

"Where'd you learn to throw? In kindergarten?" yelled Laurie.

Annie grinned. "I see that the school's ace reporter has become a sports fan," she said. Her friend Laurie was a reporter on the school newspaper.

"I just like the game," Laurie said.

"You mean you just like one of the players," Annie teased.

Annie was at least half right. Laurie did like Mike Stevens. They had been friends since they both started high school two years ago.

But Laurie really had come to watch the game. The Carver High Cubs were battling for the league championship. They had played well all season, and

they really wanted to win. Winning was a big deal in Pittsfield. Everyone in town knew that the professionals came to Pittsfield to scout new talent.

The Cubs were up against the Bay Street Pirates. The Pirates had been one of the worst teams in the league until a few months ago. Now they were in the middle of a surprise *winning* streak.

The championship had all come down to today's doubleheader between the Cubs and the Pirates. So far, the first game didn't look good for Carver.

"Bottom of the ninth," Laurie said. "One out and the game is tied at six runs each."

The next Cubs batter stepped up to home plate. "That's Joey Pearce," Laurie told Annie. "He's good."

The Pirates pitcher, Nolan Riley, looked worried. He glanced at Mike on first base. Then he looked back at the batter.

Nolan snapped a fast ball to home

plate. Joey Pearce hit a grounder that shot out past both the pitcher and the second-base player. Joey headed quickly to first base.

Meanwhile, Mike took off for second base. He barely touched the base bag before racing on to third. The crowd went wild!

The Pirates center fielder tried to catch up with the ball. When he tripped,

Joey ran full speed ahead toward second base.

The left fielder finally scooped up the ball in his mitt, but just barely.

"The Pirates couldn't catch a cold," said Annie cheerfully.

Seconds later, the left fielder sent the ball flying toward the Pirates second-base player. And Joey Pearce slid toward the base, hidden in a cloud of dust.

CHAPTER 2

The second-base player tagged Joey right before he touched the bag.

"You're out!" the umpire cried.

"I don't believe it!" Laurie shouted. A chorus of cheers and boos filled the stands. Luck was with the Pirates today!

The next Cubs batter struck out. The game was tied. It went into extra innings.

"Those Pirates are terrible fielders," Laurie grumbled. "How did they ever get this far in the league?"

Laurie glanced at the Pirates dugout. Their new coach, Amos Gaines, was pacing back and forth. His assistant, Horace Ogilvy, was near the batter's box. Ogilvy was talking to the boy on deck.

When it was his turn at bat, the boy picked up a couple of bats. He swung the bats a few times, testing their weights. Then he stepped up to the plate.

The Cubs pitcher stared coolly at the batter. Suddenly he threw a slider. There was a loud crack as the ball hit the wooden bat. The ball flew up and over the right field fence. The Pirates fans cheered loudly.

"This is getting worse by the minute," groaned Laurie. She curled her long ponytail around her fingers. In the

bottom of the tenth inning, the Cubs couldn't catch up. The Pirates won by a score of eight to six.

Laurie stood up slowly. "I have to interview the winners between games," she said to Annie. "I'll meet you and Mike in the parking lot, okay? We can eat lunch there."

Laurie made her way toward the visiting team's locker room. One of the school security guards was shooing people away.

Laurie quickly stepped back around the corner. The guard walked right by

without seeing her.

"Why am I hiding?" she asked herself. "I'm a reporter, not a fan."

Just as she was about to turn the corner, Laurie heard a door open.

"We're in the swing of it now," said a male voice. "We'll win the next game just like we won the other games."

"I told you," said a second voice. "The fix is in. The championship is all ours."

CHAPTER 3

Laurie was stunned. The Pirates were winning their games by cheating! But how were they doing it?

Laurie decided to try and get a look at the faces behind the voices she had heard. She stepped out from around the corner. But just then, the locker room door burst open.

"We're number one!" voices cheered.

Laurie found herself surrounded by the whole Pirates team.

Nolan Riley, the pitcher, was at the front of the group. "Was he one of the people I heard talking?" Laurie wondered.

Laurie recognized the boys standing next to Nolan—Tyler Moss, Robert Bell, and Cliff Addams. They were three of the Pirates' best hitters.

"Whoa," said Robert Bell. "The groupies are already waiting for us."

"In your dreams," Laurie answered him. "I just want to ask you some questions," she added. "I'm with the Carver High newspaper."

Coach Gaines interrupted them. "There won't be any interviews," he said. Then he pushed his way through the boys. He looked at Laurie suspiciously.

"Yeah," Tyler Moss said. "Can't have you giving away our little secrets."

Laurie's eyes narrowed. "I suspect *little* is the only size secret you can handle," Laurie replied angrily.

"You're just angry because we're knocking your team out of the box," Nolan Riley said.

"I've seen your best," Laurie told Nolan. "And it almost put Mike in the hospital."

"A pitch goes wild now and then," Coach Gaines explained to Laurie. "It just happens."

"Like the Pirates just happen to come up late in the season?" Laurie asked. "Is that good planning on the new coach's part? Or did you bring something else to the team?"

Coach Gaines turned his back to Laurie. "Time to go, boys," he said. "You need to rest up before the next game." The Pirates walked away with their coach, laughing and hooting.

"Ms. Chen?" Laurie turned around to find Assistant Coach Ogilvy standing in the locker room doorway.

"When you have lost everything, *anything* is worth winning," he said.

"I wrote that in one of my articles," Laurie said with some surprise.

"I read many things, including high school newspapers," Ogilvy told her. "It's a very good way to learn about the other teams."

"Anything to help the Pirates win, eh?" Laurie said.

"Of course I want to be helpful. I've been with the team for nine years," Ogilvy replied.

"Then why weren't you made head coach when the old coach retired?" Laurie asked.

"I'm not tough enough," sighed Ogilvy.

"And Coach Gaines is?" asked Laurie.

"Ex-marines usually are," Ogilvy said softly. "To Gaines, winning is everything."

"Is it worth cheating?" Laurie asked.

Ogilvy sighed again. "Have a nice day, Ms. Chen," he said. Then he turned sharply and walked away.

Laurie shook her head. She went off in search of Mike and Annie.

Laurie wasted no time telling her friends what she had heard outside the Pirates locker room.

"I'd like to believe the Pirates

cheated," Mike said when Laurie finished her story. "Their hitters really creamed us." Then he frowned. "But I know some of those guys. They're okay."

"Maybe," Laurie said thoughtfully. She stopped next to her old, beat-up bicycle.

As Mike reached into the bike basket for a sandwich, Laurie suddenly froze. She had spotted something from the corner of her eye. A large blur was racing toward her head. And it was coming at incredible speed!

CHAPTER 4

Laurie ducked just before the object struck. It shattered the driver's window of a car that was parked nearby. Then it rolled across the ground.

"It's a baseball!" Laurie gasped. Her hand was trembling as she picked it up.

"Are you all right?" Annie cried out. "That ball could have killed you!"

Laurie nodded. She was a little shaken, but okay.

Mike glanced around the parking lot. "Whoever threw that ball knew exactly what he was doing," he said.

"Nolan Riley would know," Laurie said. "If he's cheating somehow, he wouldn't want me snooping around."

"But how does someone fix a ball

game anyway?" Annie asked.

"You could pay off an umpire. Or maybe you could rig the equipment," Mike suggested.

"Or you could bribe players on one of the teams," Laurie added. She stared hard at Mike.

"No one on the Cubs would throw the game!" Mike shouted back at her. "We all want to win too much. And some of us need sports scholarships to make it into college."

"I know," Laurie said. "But the Pirates have fixed this game somehow."

"Suppose they did bribe a Cubs player? That means they have paid off someone on each team they played," Mike argued.

Annie whistled. "That's a lot of money!"

"Too much," Laurie agreed. "There has to be another way they're cheating." She looked thoughtful.

"I'm going over to the *Pittsfield*

Gazette," Laurie decided. "I want to read about the Pirates' last few games."

"Okay," said Mike. "But be careful!"

Laurie gave him a peck on the cheek. Then she and Annie jumped onto their bikes and pedaled down to the newspaper office.

The Pirates' sudden success had made them a real news item. For half an hour, the two girls pored over news clippings and photos. There was even a full-color picture of the team. Each player was holding either a ball, a mitt, or a shiny

metal bat. Everyone, even Coach Gaines, was smiling. Assistant Coach Ogilvy was at the edge of the picture. Part of him had been cut off.

"Always in the background," Laurie muttered. She stared at the picture for a moment. Suddenly something caught her attention.

"Find something?" asked Annie.

"Maybe," Laurie answered.

Laurie lined up all the pictures next to each other. In the team shots, the Pirates batters were holding metal bats. But the bats were different in the pictures taken during the games.

Laurie looked at her watch. "The second game has already started. We've got to hurry back!" she insisted.

"But . . ." Annie started to answer.

"I'll explain on the way," Laurie said.

CHAPTER 5

By the time Laurie and Annie reached the ballpark, it was already the top of the second inning. The scoreboard read: PIRATES 1, CUBS 0.

"Go get Security," Laurie told Annie.

Then she ran over to the Cubs dugout. Mike was standing there with his coach.

"Did Tyler, Robert, or Cliff hit that run on the scoreboard?" Laurie asked.

"Cliff did," Mike replied. "Why?"

"Because those three players hit most of the runs yesterday," Laurie explained. "And at every game the Pirates have won since Coach Gaines took over."

Laurie watched as Tyler Moss approached the batter's box. He was swinging two bats. One was made of wood, the other of aluminum.

"You use an aluminum bat, right?" Laurie asked Mike.

"Yeah, everybody does," he answered.

"Not Tyler, or Cliff, or Robert," Laurie said. "They all use the same wooden bat every time they come up to the plate."

Mike and Laurie watched Tyler throw the aluminum bat aside.

"See?" she said. Laurie ran toward home plate. Mike was right behind her.

"Grab that bat!" she yelled. Tyler Moss was startled. He threw down his bat and began to run for the far gate.

"Stop him!" Laurie shouted. She picked up the bat and handed it to the umpire.

Mike chased Tyler and tackled him just before he reached the gate. Players from both teams charged out of the dugouts. For a moment it looked like there was going to be a rumble. But the coaches quickly calmed everyone down.

Laurie was the first person to reach

Mike and Tyler.

"It wasn't my idea!" Tyler shouted.

"What wasn't?" Mike asked.

"Using a nonregulation bat," said the umpire. He held up Tyler's wooden bat. "The center has been drilled out. It's packed with cork. That's illegal."

"Who rigged that bat?" Laurie asked.

Tyler looked at Robert Bell. Robert looked at Cliff Addams. All three boys looked at Horace Ogilvy.

"Strike three for me," Ogilvy said sadly. "I did it. Only these three boys knew. Then I worked out the batting lineup. I figured after we won the championship, everyone would think my batting lineup saved the day. And then next year I would get the head coach contract."

"You wanted my job that much?" Coach Gaines asked.

Ogilvy turned to Gaines. "It should have been my job," Ogilvy said, almost to himself. "Yes, I wanted it that much."

"Is that why you pitched that speed ball at my head?" Laurie asked.

Ogilvy glared at Laurie. "There was a lot of money at stake! The boys and I had bets on the Pirates. I only meant to scare you off." Ogilvy lowered his head. "Now I've lost everything," he muttered.

"Including your honor," Laurie added.

"And the team's honor, too," Nolan Riley said angrily.

"The bat is out of the game, and so are these three boys," said the head umpire. "Cliff's run comes off the scoreboard. We'll talk about penalties later. If the Cubs win this game, there'll be a tie-breaker tomorrow."

A security guard led Horace Ogilvy and the three boys off the field. Coach Gaines asked for time out. He needed to talk to his players.

Mike and Laurie headed off the field.

"How did you figure it all out?" Mike asked Laurie.

"Remember what I heard near the locker room? 'We're in the swing of it now'?" Laurie explained. "And remember what you said about rigging equipment? Well, I'd been watching those guys at bat. And like a good reporter, I checked the newspapers!" Laurie grinned. "I just didn't know Ogilvy was behind it all."

"You did great," Mike said. "Now we have a real, *fair* shot at winning the championship. So, see you after the game?" he asked shyly.

Laurie smiled. "If you win," she teased.

"Watch my smoke!" Mike laughed. Then he ran off to the dugout.

The umpire yelled, "Play ball!"